# Old Testament

# Scripture Sleuth

**Written by**

Alyson Kieda

**Illustrations and Cover Design by**

Elizabeth Adams

*Publisher*
In Celebration™
a division of Instructional Fair • TS Denison
Grand Rapids, Michigan

## Permission to Reproduce

## How to Use the Book

*Scripture Sleuth* is a game that challenges students to learn about the Bible in a new, creative way. Each day, the teacher provides a new clue, beginning with the most general and difficult. As the week progresses, the clues become more specific and familiar. Participants may use a Bible or concordance to research the clues. The object of the game is to use the daily clues to discover the name of the mystery person, place, or event of the Old Testament. The teacher may design a permanent bulletin board for displaying *Scripture Sleuth* clues. A new clue replaces or is added to the clues on the board every day. On Monday, "Last Week's *Scripture Sleuth* Answer" is displayed. A *Scripture Sleuth* Award may be given to all who (or the first person to) successfully solve the mystery. As variations, a clue could be provided weekly or the game could be played in one sitting. The game may be used in a classroom, a Bible club, a youth group, at home, or in many other settings.

## About the Author

*Alyson Kieda* has been an editor with Instructional Fair • TS Denison for over three years. Prior to this, she worked as an editor and proofreader for several Christian publishers and a local university. In the past, Alyson also enjoyed editing and writing for a Christian magazine, several Christian newsletters, and a camp newsletter. She currently resides near Grand Rapids, Michigan, with her husband and three children.

## Credits

Author: Alyson Kieda
Illustrator: Elizabeth Adams
Cover Artist: Elizabeth Adams
Project Director/Editor: Alyson Kieda
Editors: Rhonda DeWaard, Lisa Hancock
Typesetting/Layout: Pat Geasler

*Melissa Atwood*

# Table of Contents

## The Garden of Eden

**Monday**

This beautiful place was located at the point where one river divides into four rivers.

**Tuesday**

This place contained pretty trees that grew wholesome fruit.

**Wednesday**

Angels later guarded this place with a flaming sword.

**Thursday**

In this place, a man and a woman tried to hide from God.

**Friday**

A man gave names to all the animals that lived in this place.

## Last Week's Scripture Sleuth Answer

When God created Adam and Eve, he placed them in the beautiful **Garden of Eden**. This garden provided everything they could want. All God asked was that they not eat from the tree of the knowledge of good and evil. One day, the devil, disguised as a snake, tempted the woman to eat a piece of fruit from the tree. The woman, in turn, tempted her husband to eat. After this, the man and woman realized that what they had done was wrong and tried to clothe themselves and hide from God. For their disobedience, they were expelled from the garden. God placed cherubim with a flaming sword on the east side of the garden to guard the tree of life.

*Read the complete story in Genesis 2–3.*

Noah

This man lived to the ripe old age of 950.

When God observed the people he had created, only this man pleased him.

God told this man to build a large structure out of cypress wood.

**Thursday**

This man and his family gathered pairs of animals and loaded them into a large boat.

**Friday**

This man and his family were aboard an ark with animals of every kind while it rained for 40 days and nights.

## Last Week's Scripture Sleuth Answer

Some time after God had created man, God was sorry that he had done so. All God could see was wickedness everywhere. Only **Noah** found favor with God. God decided to destroy the earth and spare only Noah; his wife; Noah's sons, Shem, Ham, and Japheth; and his sons' wives. God instructed Noah to build a great ark and then to gather pairs of animals of every kind. After the ark was finished and the animals were on board, the rain began. It rained for 40 days and nights.

A few months later, after the water had receded, the ark came to rest on a mountain. Noah sent out a raven and then a dove. The dove returned because there was no place to land. A week later he sent it out again and it returned with an olive leaf. Soon after, the people and animals were able to leave the ark. In thanks, Noah offered burnt offerings to God. In turn, God promised to never again destroy the earth with a flood. He gave Noah the rainbow as a sign of this promise.

*Read more in Genesis 5–9.*

Abraham

Monday

This man was visited by three angels.

Tuesday

God asked him to sacrifice his son.

Wednesday

God called this man to leave his people and his country and to journey to another country.

**Thursday**

God promised this man that his offspring would be as numerous as the stars in the heavens.

**Friday**

This man and his wife, Sarah, were very old when they became parents.

## Last Week's Scripture Sleuth Answer

**Abraham** means "father of many." Abraham was 75 when God called him to leave his country and people to go to the land of Canaan, where God would bless him. Abraham departed with his wife, Sarah, his nephew Lot, and Lot's family. Although Abraham and Sarah were already old, God promised that their offspring would be too many to count. Finally, after several years, Abraham and Sarah were blessed with the birth of Isaac.

*Read Abraham's story in Genesis 12–25.*

Sarah

When this woman was 127, she died and was buried in a cave in the land of Canaan.

Tuesday

She married her half brother.

Wednesday

She was such a beautiful woman that two rulers tried to add her to their harems.

**Thursday**

This woman laughed in disbelief when she overheard an angel say that she would soon have a son. She was much too old!

**Friday**

She was 90 when she gave birth to her first and only son, Isaac.

## Last Week's Scripture Sleuth Answer

Sarah set out with her husband, Abraham, when he was called to leave everything and journey to Canaan. God made a promise to Abraham that his descendants would be too many to count. When Sarah did not get pregnant, she gave Abraham her maidservant, in hopes that she would have a son and that this would fulfill God's promise. Later, Sarah was in a tent when she overheard an angel tell Abraham that Sarah would soon have a son. She laughed. How could she possibly have a son when she and her husband were both so old? Yet God fulfilled his promise. Sarah gave birth to Isaac, whose name means "laughter."

*Read Sarah's story in Genesis 12–23.*

IF9575 *Scripture Sleuth–Old Testament*

Joseph

This man's brothers did not recognize him.

Tuesday

He spent several years as a servant of the captain of the guard.

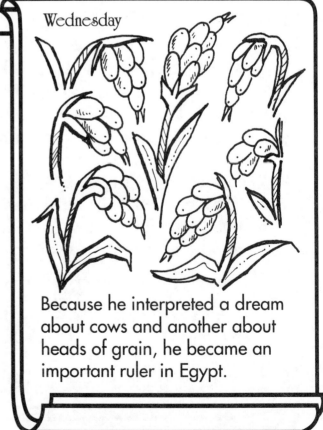

Wednesday

Because he interpreted a dream about cows and another about heads of grain, he became an important ruler in Egypt.

**Thursday**

This man's jealous brothers sold him to some merchants headed for Egypt.

**Friday**

His father, Jacob, loved him so much that he gave him a richly ornamented coat.

## Last Week's Scripture Sleuth Answer

**Joseph** was the son of Jacob and Rachel. Jacob loved Joseph more than any of his sons. Because of this and Joseph's dreams in which he ruled over them, his brothers were extremely jealous. One day his brothers threw him into a well and sold him to some passing merchants. The brothers took Joseph's robe, dipped it in goat's blood, and gave it to Jacob saying that a wild animal had killed him. Joseph became a slave in Potiphar's house. Joseph faithfully served for several years until Potiphar's wife falsely accused him and he was thrown into prison. While in prison, Joseph interpreted the dreams of Pharaoh's butler and baker. Two years later, when the Pharaoh was troubled by two dreams, the butler remembered Joseph and recommended him to Pharaoh. Joseph interpreted the dreams and Pharaoh rewarded him by making him second in command. Seven years of plentiful harvests, in which Joseph stockpiled grain for the future, were followed by seven years of famine. During the famine, Jacob sent his sons to Egypt to buy grain. Joseph forgave his brothers and all his family was relocated to Egypt.

*Read Genesis 37–50 to learn more.*

Moses

Monday

This man let his brother do the talking.

Tuesday

After being with God, this man's face shone.

Wednesday

He led his people to a land that he was not allowed to enter.

**Thursday**

When he was a baby, he was laid in a waterproof basket and placed among the reeds of the Nile River.

**Friday**

This man went up to a mountain for 40 days and came back down with the Ten Commandments.

## Last Week's Scripture Sleuth Answer

God captured **Moses'** attention by calling out to him from a burning bush. He told Moses he was sending him to Pharaoh to demand the release of the Israelites. Moses did not feel that he was a good speaker, so God agreed to let Moses' brother Aaron talk for him. Moses was 80 when he and Aaron spoke with Pharoah. After several requests and 10 terrible plagues, Pharoah finally let the people go. Moses led the people to Mt. Sinai, where he met with God and received the law and the Ten Commandments. While Moses was away, the people strayed. As a result of this and many other sins, the people were forced to wander in the desert for 40 years. Moses finally brought them to the Promised Land where he glimpsed the land of Canaan before he died.

*Read about Moses and the Israelites in Exodus through Deuteronomy.*

The Passover

This is an important Jewish feast.

This event takes place in the first month of the Hebrew calendar, called Nisan.

The Egyptians did not celebrate this feast.

**Thursday**

On this night, God spared the Israelites from a terrible event.

**Friday**

This event signifies the beginning of the Israelites' deliverance from slavery in Egypt.

## Last Week's Scripture Sleuth Answer

God gave detailed directions to Moses about the preparation for the **Passover**. Each household was to take the blood of a lamb and spread it on the tops and sides of its door frames. The people then ate an evening meal of lamb with bitter herbs and unleavened bread. That same night, God went through Egypt striking down all the first-born. God would pass over any house with a doorway marked with blood. After this tenth devastating plague, Pharaoh let the Israelites go. The Passover feast continues to be observed today as "a festival to the Lord" (Exodus 12:14).

*Read about the first Passover in Exodus 12.*

The Exodus

Monday

The bones of Joseph were moved during this event.

Tuesday

A book of the Bible bears the same name as this event.

Wednesday

This event delivered a people from years of bondage.

**Thursday**

During this event, a pillar of cloud separated the Israelites from their enemies.

**Friday**

During this daring escape, the people walked through a parted sea.

# Last Week's Scripture Sleuth Answer

An exodus is a departure of a whole group of people. In the Old Testament **exodus,** God used Moses to deliver the Israelites from years of cruel slavery under the Egyptians. Moses, with brother Aaron speaking, went to Pharaoh to convince him to let the people go. After much persuading (in the form of 10 plagues), Pharaoh relented and said they could go. After the people left, Pharaoh changed his mind and pursued them. During the exodus, God used miraculous means to enable the Israelites to escape. God provided a pillar of cloud at night to prevent the Egyptians from seeing them and then parted the Red Sea so the people could cross over. The Egyptians followed and were swallowed up by the waters. During the people's wanderings, God continued to provide for all their needs until they were allowed to enter the Promised Land.

*The story of the exodus begins in Exodus and ends in Joshua as the people conquer and enter the Promised Land.*

Jericho

**Monday**

This city lies about 1,000 feet below sea level.

**Tuesday**

Archaeological evidence suggests that this is one of the oldest cities in the world.

**Wednesday**

A woman named Rahab was spared when this city was destroyed.

**Thursday**

This was the first Canaanite city taken by the invading Israelites.

**Friday**

The walls of this city fell when trumpets blew and an army, led by Joshua, shouted.

## Last Week's Scripture Sleuth Answer

Jericho was a large and thriving city that lay in the Promised Land (Canaan). Joshua sent two spies into Jericho to look over the land. While there, the spies stayed with a prostitute named Rahab. Rahab hid them and then let them down over the city walls by a rope through her window. For her information and generous aid, Rahab received a promise that she and all her family would be spared when the city was destroyed. When the spies relayed all that they had seen and heard, Joshua was convinced that they should conquer the land. His conviction was confirmed when an angel appeared and told him how to overtake the city. For six days, all the armed men marched around the city once each day. On the seventh day, the men, preceded by seven priests bearing trumpets and the ark, marched around the city six times. On the seventh time around, when the priests blew their trumpets and Joshua gave the command, the army shouted and the walls of the city collapsed. Only Rahab and her family were spared.

*Read about the city of Jericho in Joshua 2–6.*

Ruth

This woman gathered grain in the field of her future husband.

This woman left her family, friends, and land in order to follow her mother-in-law to Bethlehem.

This woman was the great-grandmother of King David.

**Thursday**

This woman is one of two women with a book of the Bible bearing her name.

**Friday**

This woman's mother-in-law was Naomi.

## Last Week's Scripture Sleuth Answer

Naomi and her family moved to Moab when famine struck Bethlehem. While there, her two sons married Moabite women. **Ruth** was married to one of Naomi's two sons. After Naomi's husband and her two sons died, Naomi decided to return to Bethlehem. She set out with her daughters-in-law but then convinced one to return. After all, she reasoned, she could not hope to provide sons for them to marry. Ruth begged to follow Naomi and pledged that "your people will be my people and your God my God" (Ruth 1:16).

While in Bethlehem, Ruth proved to be the model daughter-in-law. She went to glean grain in the field of Boaz, a relation of Naomi's husband. Ruth gained Boaz's favor through her devotion to her mother-in-law and for her wisdom in following God. Boaz petitioned with the next of kin to marry her. The nearest kinsman relinquished his right to marry Ruth. Ruth and Boaz married and had a son, Obed, the grandfather of King David.

*Read more about Ruth in the Book of Ruth.*

**David**

Monday

He was a very handsome youth. He is described as "ruddy, with a fine appearance and handsome features."

Tuesday

He is known for his strength and courage. When he was young, he killed bears and lions who tried to attack the sheep he tended for his father.

Wednesday

He played the harp for King Saul when Saul was troubled. His playing would often soothe the king.

**Thursday**

When he was a boy, he defeated a Philistine giant with just a slingshot and a stone.

**Friday**

This man became the second king of Israel and ruled for over 40 years. His son, Solomon, became the next king.

## Last Week's Scripture Sleuth Answer

**David** was the youngest son of Jesse. One day while David was tending his father's sheep, his father asked him to bring supplies to three of his brothers in the army. David was disturbed to see and hear Goliath's taunts and volunteered to fight against this nine-foot-tall giant. Armed with only a slingshot and a few stones, he defeated the boastful giant. About this same time, David began to play the harp for King Saul and at some point became King Saul's armor bearer. Over time, David earned a high rank in Saul's army. When the people began to sing David's praises, Saul became very jealous and tried to kill him. David fled. After Saul died, David became king.

Despite David's later sins and shortcomings, he is considered Israel's most important king. During his reign, Israel reached the height of its power and influence. David achieved many military victories. He also brought the ark into Jerusalem, a cause for much rejoicing. He is credited with writing 73 of the psalms.

*Read the story of David in 1 Samuel 16–1 Kings 2.*

Esther

**Monday**

Her Jewish name was Hadassah, which in Hebrew means "myrtle."

**Tuesday**

She helped save her people from being massacred.

**Wednesday**

This woman's husband chose her because of her great beauty.

**Thursday**

This woman was raised by her cousin Mordecai.

**Friday**

She was a queen of Persia. Her husband's name was Xerxes.

## Last Week's Scripture Sleuth Answer

**Esther** became the queen of Persia after the former queen was expelled for refusing to obey her husband's command to parade before his banquet guests. King Xerxes chose Esther because, of all the beautiful women brought before him, her beauty surpassed them all. When she became queen, Mordecai advised Esther to keep her Jewish heritage a secret. This proved to be wise advice. During this same time, a man named Haman was given a high position among the nobles. Because Mordecai would not bow down to Haman, Haman plotted to destroy the Jews. Through Esther's obedience to God and her daring actions, her people, the Jews, were saved and Haman was hanged. Mordecai then became second in command to King Xerxes.

*Read about Esther in the Book of Esther.*

Daniel

MENE MENE TEKEL

This man was known for his wisdom and his uncanny ability to interpret dreams.

Tuesday

Thou Shall Not PRAY

He disobeyed a decree and continued to pray to God.

Wednesday

His enemies tried to have him removed from office but could not because "he was trustworthy and neither corrupt nor negligent."

**Thursday**

This man's three friends, Shadrach, Meshach, and Abednego, were thrown into a fiery furnace.

**Friday**

He was thrown into a lions' den and came out alive!

# Last Week's Scripture Sleuth Answer

Daniel was among a select group of Israelite men who were brought to the Babylonian king Nebuchadnezzar's palace after Jerusalem was besieged. These men were educated for three years in the king's courts. God gave them knowledge and wisdom, and Daniel was also given the ability to understand visions and dreams. Twice, with God's help, Daniel interpreted the king's dreams. Later, Daniel interpreted mysterious writing on the wall for Nebuchadnezzar's son King Belshazzar. Each time, Daniel was rewarded with a high government position. When Darius became king, Daniel again was given a high position.

Throughout the years, Daniel continued to give thanks to God as he had always done. When Daniel's enemies failed to find any grounds for expelling him from office, they convinced King Darius to make an edict that anyone who prayed to any but the king would be thrown into the lions' den. Though Daniel was thrown into the den, God kept the lions from devouring him.

*Read about Daniel in the Book of Daniel.*

Jonah

NINEVEH

TARSISH OR BUST

God called this man to go to a wicked place to preach against the people's evil deeds. Instead of obeying, he tried to run away.

Tuesday

This man was angry at God because God did not destroy the wicked city of Nineveh.

Wednesday

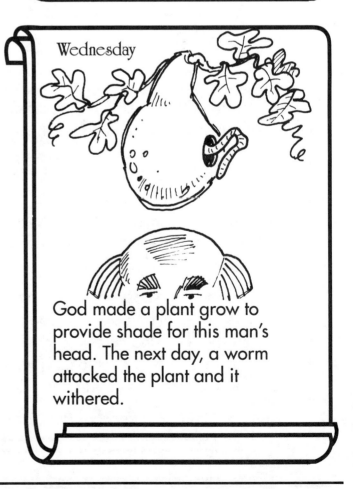

God made a plant grow to provide shade for this man's head. The next day, a worm attacked the plant and it withered.

**Thursday**

After a violent storm began, sailors threw this man overboard.

**Friday**

BURP

This prophet was swallowed by a huge fish and remained in its belly for three days.

## Last Week's Scripture Sleuth Answer

God called **Jonah** to go to the city of Nineveh to preach against the wickedness of the people. Instead of obeying, Jonah tried to flee by boarding a ship bound for Tarshish. While Jonah slept, God caused a great storm to violently rock the ship. Jonah, aware that he was at fault for the storm, asked the sailors to throw him overboard. At his insistence, they did. Immediately, the storm subsided. Jonah was swallowed by a great fish, where he remained for three days. During that time, Jonah prayed. The fish spit up Jonah on dry land.

This time, Jonah obeyed and went to Nineveh. After hearing Jonah's words, the people of Nineveh were repentant and God spared them. Jonah was angry at God for not destroying them. He went east of the city, built a shelter, and sat, hoping to see God destroy the city. While he waited, God caused a plant to grow over the shelter to provide shade. The next day a worm attacked and killed the plant. God used this event to teach Jonah an important lesson about his compassion for all people.

*Read the entire story in the Book of Jonah.*

Scripture Sleuth Award

Congratulations to

_____

for successfully solving
the Old Testament mystery person
place, or event

on this day _____